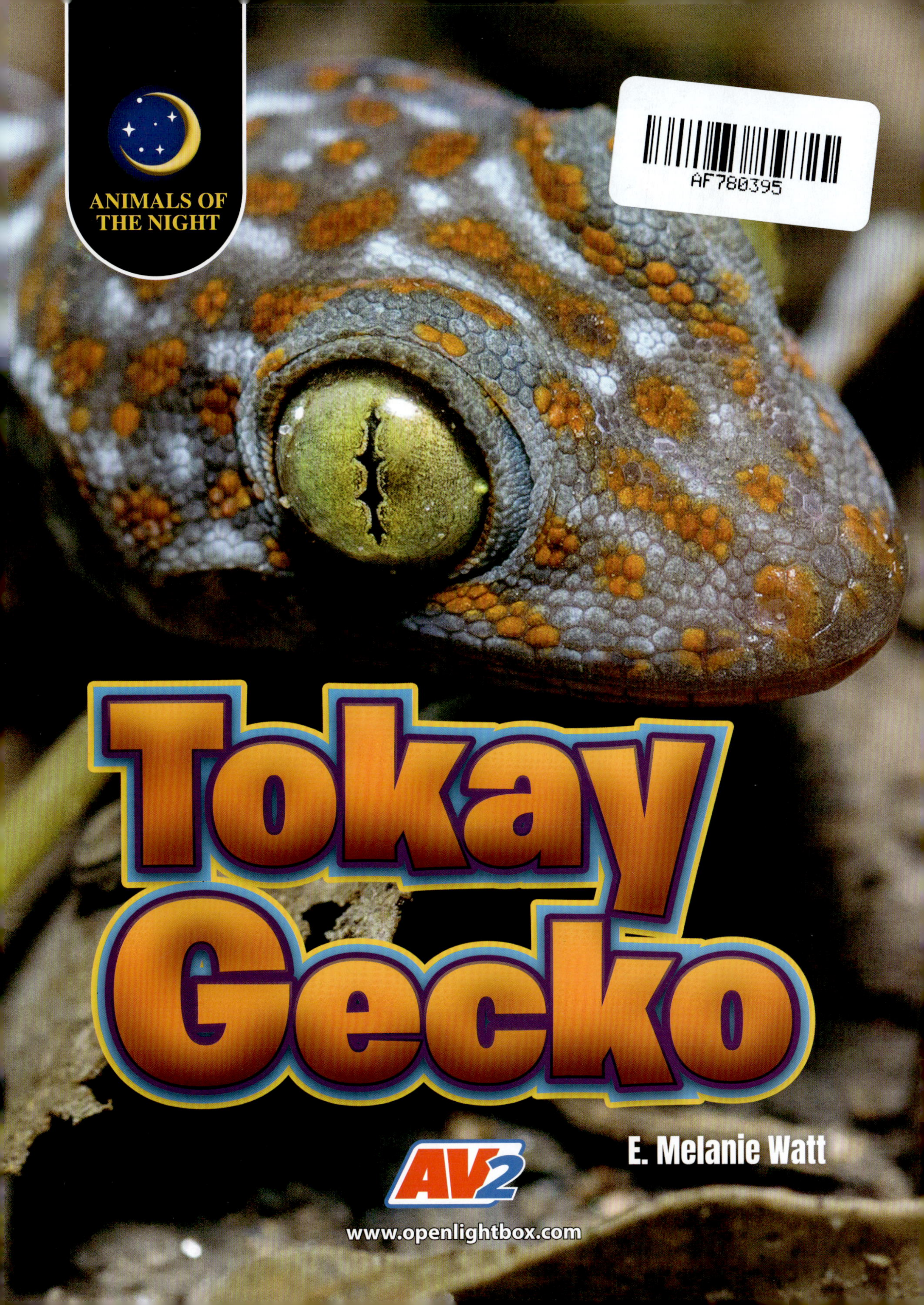

ANIMALS OF THE NIGHT

Tokay Gecko

E. Melanie Watt

AV2
www.openlightbox.com

1-Year Grades K–5 Subscription
ISBN 978-1-7911-3320-7

ANIMALS OF THE NIGHT

Tokay Gecko

Contents

The Tokay Gecko

People can see straight through a tokay gecko's head by looking into one ear hole and out through the other.

Tokay geckos are spotted reptiles. They are known for their thick, cylinder-shaped bodies, big heads, and large eyes. As part of the gecko group of **lizards**, tokays are known for their ability to climb walls. Their name comes from the "to-kay" sound of their calls. These sharp-toothed **predators** feed on insects and other small animals. Tokays are **nocturnal** animals, meaning that they hunt at night using senses adapted for the darkness.

Tokay Gecko Facts

Weighing up to **0.9 pounds** (400 grams), the tokay gecko is one of the world's **largest** geckos.

Tokay geckos can **dangle** from a surface using just **one toe**.

A tokay gecko has a small **"third eye"** on its forehead. The eye cannot see, but can sense light.

What Is a Gecko?

The tokay is only one of about 2,000 species of geckos known today. More than one third of all known lizard species are geckos. Geckos can be many different shapes, sizes, and colors. Most have well-developed legs with feet that can cling to almost any surface. Geckos have thick tails that store fat and help with balance when climbing or lunging. Geckos can also drop off their tails to escape predators and then grow new ones. Like other lizards, geckos shed the outer layer of their skin as they grow.

Instead of movable eyelids, many geckos, including tokays, have a transparent lens over each eye that protects it and keeps it moist. The lizards lick this lens to keep it clean. Unlike most other lizards, geckos are known to make vocal sounds. Most gecko species make different sounds. They chirp, click, and bark to attract mates and defend their territories.

Comparing Geckos

	Tokay Gecko	Virgin Gorda Least Gecko	Yellow-Headed Day Gecko	Western Banded Gecko
Length including tail	8 to 16 inches (20 to 41 centimeters)	1.2 inches (3 cm)	3.3 to 3.75 inches (8.4 to 9.5 cm)	4 to 6 inches (10 to 15 cm)
Weight	5.3 to 14.1 ounces (150 to 400 g)	0.0015 to 0.0053 ounces (0.04 to 0.15 g)	0.06 ounces (1.7 g)	0.16 ounces (4.56 g)
Diet	**Invertebrates** including locusts, moths, cockroaches, and spiders, as well as small **mammals**, birds, and reptiles	Very small invertebrates, including mites	Insects and nectar	Invertebrates including beetles, spiders, grasshoppers, sowbugs, and termites
Habitat	Subtropical and tropical moist lowlands, mountain forests	Subtropical and tropical dry scrublands, rocky hillsides	Subtropical and tropical dry and moist lowland forests	Grasslands, deserts

Geckos are found in many different **habitats**. They live in warm areas on every continent except Antarctica. Like other reptiles, they are cold-blooded, meaning their bodies produce very little heat, so their body temperature depends on their surrounding environment. Although some gecko species are **diurnal**, about 72 percent are nocturnal. Nocturnal geckos can see and hunt well in low light.

A Closer Look

A tokay gecko's unique adaptations help it survive in its habitat in many different ways. Some help the gecko find and catch **prey**, while others allow it to protect itself from threats.

Tail When tokays cast off their tail, they do so at one of several different sections. The tail moves around on its own for several minutes, distracting a predator. Tokay tails grow back after about three weeks.

Skin The blue-gray skin on a tokay gecko's body is covered in red, orange, yellow, or black spots.. This helps provide **camouflage**. Tokays can also lighten or darken their skin to blend into their environment.

Teeth Tokay geckos have sharp teeth and powerful jaws. They use their powerful bites to catch prey, fight off predators, and defend their territory from rivals. This includes other tokays.

Eyes Large, light-sensitive **pupils** help tokays see at night. In daylight, the pupils narrow to a vertical slit. This reduces the amount of light entering a gecko's eyes, protecting them.

Feet A tokay gecko's feet cling to most surfaces with the help of millions of tiny hair-like objects called setae. Tokay geckos can attach to and release from surfaces quickly, which makes them able to rapidly climb as they move.

Tokay Gecko Diet

★★ Tokays stay very still after catching their prey. This helps them avoid predators while they feed.

Tokay geckos mostly eat invertebrates, including insects and spiders. However, they also hunt small animals such as mice, snakes, and birds. Tokay geckos come out of their daytime resting places to hunt alone at night, using their vision. They also have a strong sense of hearing and are able to smell and "taste" scent particles in the air using their tongues.

A tokay gecko mainly hunts by **ambushing** its prey. The lizard waits for a small animal to come close. Then, it lunges forward and attacks. This sit-and-wait hunting strategy means tokay geckos spend very little energy catching prey.

Food Chain

When an animal eats a plant or animal, it takes in energy from its food. Food chains show this movement of energy.

Producer
Grass

Primary consumer
Locust

Tokay Gecko Facts

The grip of a tokay gecko's feet can hold about **450 pounds** (204 kilograms) of weight.

Tokay geckos **do not chew** small prey. They eat it in **one bite**.

A tokay gecko has **about 100 teeth**.

Secondary Consumer
Tokay Gecko

Tertiary Consumer
Golden Tree Snake

Behavior

Tokay geckos are very difficult for predators or prey to see on trees or in other parts of their environment. Extra skin folds on their bodies help prevent them from casting a shadow when they lie flat on a surface. When a tokay gecko is resting, the folds spread out to help flatten the lizard's shape even more. This means that tokays are able to spend most of the day hidden from threats while they rest.

Tokay geckos make a variety of noises, some of which can be heard dozens of feet (meters) away. Male tokay geckos attract females with low cackles followed by their "to-kay" call. Females make a similar, higher-pitched noise.

If a tokay gecko is cornered by a predator, or is protecting its territory, eggs, or young, it will defend itself. Both male and female tokay geckos may aggressively hiss or hold their mouths open and bark. If the threat does not leave, tokays will strike. Their mouths snap shut quickly in a powerful bite that is strong enough to draw blood from humans.

Tokay geckos make sounds by rubbing sacs in their throats together.

An adult tokay gecko usually sheds its skin about once every four to six weeks.

Tokay geckos protect their territories from both each other and other types of animals. By doing so, the lizard avoids having to compete for food in its home area.

Life Cycle

The tokay gecko mating season is a 4- to 5-month period. It typically lasts between October and May. A female gecko will lay two eggs each month and attach them to a surface within her mate's territory. The eggs are guarded by both parents until they hatch.

Hatchling Eggs in the same spot will hatch at different times, depending on when they were laid. The hatchlings emerge 3 to 6 months after their eggs are laid. Newly hatched tokay geckos are only about 2 to 3 inches (5.1 to 7.6 cm) long, and weigh about 0.08 ounces (2.3 g). They first depend on an attached yolk sac for nutrition. As they grow, they begin eating small insects.

Juvenile A tokay gecko's diet depends on the size of its body. Juveniles eat larger insects than hatchlings, but feed on smaller prey than adults. Parents continue to protect juveniles. The young lizards remain with their parents until they are 10 to 12 months old.

Adult Tokays are still growing quickly while they are between 1 and 2 years of age. At this time, both male and female tokay geckos are able to have young of their own. They reach adult size when they are about 2 years old. Male tokay geckos tend to be larger and more brightly colored than females. A tokay gecko's lifespan is about 10 years, but some can live up to 20.

Habitats

Tokay geckos are native to countries including China, India, Indonesia, Malaysia, the Philippines, Thailand, and Vietnam. These geckos have also been introduced to other parts of the world due to human activity. Some are moved through the traditional medicine and pet trades. Others arrive in new countries accidentally when they hide in cargo shipments.

The tokay gecko's natural habitats are subtropical and tropical forests. These lizards spend most of their time in trees. Tokays also thrive in artificial environments created by people, such as farms, as long as they have enough food and shelter. During the day, tokay geckos are typically found resting in trees or in cracks in rocks and buildings.

1. Hawaii, United States

Hawaii is one of the places in which tokay **populations** are not naturally found. However, a population of the lizards now lives there. They are considered to be an **invasive species** and harmful to local wildlife. Hawaii's tokay gecko population was likely the result of escaped or released pets.

2. Barail Wildlife Sanctuary, India

One of the larger wildlife sanctuaries in the state of Assam, this 126-square-mile (326-square-kilometer) sanctuary was established in 2004. It protects many plants and animals, including India's native tokay geckos.

3. Khao Yai National Park, Thailand

Founded in 1962, Khao Yai National Park is Thailand's oldest national park. The park includes rainforests and grasslands. More than 85 different reptile species, including the tokay gecko, call the park home.

Tokay Geckos and People

Tokay geckos and people interact in many ways. Unlike many animals, tokay geckos adapt well to human settlements, and can be found in homes in populated areas. In some cultures, they are considered welcome visitors.

Many people like having tokay geckos on their property because the lizards hunt household pests each night. Some people even trap tokays from forests and release them on their property in hopes that the lizards will stay. Tokay geckos continue to be culturally important in many Asian countries in part because of the myths and legends that surround them.

One reason why tokay geckos have adapted well to human development is that the insects they eat are attracted to lights.

Myths and Legends

In parts of Asia, tokay geckos are thought to have descended from dragons and have supernatural powers.

Myth 1

In Bali, Indonesia, some believe geckos are "Home Gods" and that having geckos in their homes protect the buildings from bad things outside. Many who do not believe in "Home Gods" still think that geckos bring goodness and luck. It is often believed that killing a tokay gecko will bring bad luck.

Myth 2

Tokay geckos are used in traditional Asian medicines. Some people believe that parts of the lizards can help treat a wide range of ailments, including cancer and diabetes. At different times, this has led huge numbers of tokays to be killed for use in medicine. However, these medicinal claims are not supported by scientific evidence.

Conservation

★ Tokay geckos are considered a species of least concern. This means they are not considered to be threatened with extinction globally.

Millions of tokay geckos are caught for different reasons each year. Besides being killed for use in traditional medicine, tokays are also trapped for the pet trade because of their large size and color. They are often hunted for food as well. Although tokay geckos are a common species, in some areas, such as China, populations have greatly decreased over recent years. Thailand exports about 2 to 5 million tokay geckos a year to countries including China, Malaysia, and the United States. Indonesia exports 1.2 million dead and dried tokays per year.

The Convention on International Trade in Endangered Species of Wild Fauna and Flora (CITES) is an agreement between more than 150 countries to protect plants and animals that are traded internationally. Due to uncontrolled hunting of tokay geckos in many places, the species was included in the 2019 Appendix II of CITES. This means the trade of these lizards must be controlled to protect their population.

Activity

Many issues facing tokay geckos today are similar to those facing other species of wildlife.

1. Pick one of the issues below. Research it using this book, the internet, and the library.
2. Read the research questions in the concept web on this page. Use the relationships between concepts to help you define your point of view on the issue.
3. Once your research is completed, explain your point of view on the issue.

Issues

Unproven Treatments

Millions of tokay geckos and many other wildlife species, including elephants, tigers, and bears, are killed each year. Their parts are used in traditional medicines.

Foreign Invasive Species

Human activities, including trade of live animals, have caused tokay geckos to become invasive species in areas they are not native to, with consequences on natural ecosystems.

Population Declines

Although tokay geckos are not considered to be endangered, their numbers have declined greatly in some countries as they are taken from nature.

Concept Web

Issue Name

- Which pieces of information helped you form your opinion on this issue?
- What historical events have impacted this issue? How?
- What other people would be affected by the issue? Which people would it impact the most?
- Should there be laws in your country relating to this issue? Why or why not?
- Could you be affected in the future by this issue? How?
- Which groups or individuals would support or disagree with your stance? Why?

Tokay Gecko Quiz

1 What percentage of gecko species are nocturnal?

2 How do tokays clean their eye lenses?

3 How many species of gecko are known today?

4 How can a tokay's tail distract predators?

5 What shape is the pupil in a tokay's eye during daylight?

6 How do tokay geckos make sounds?

7 How long do tokay eggs take to hatch after they are laid?

8 Up to how many pounds can a tokay gecko weigh?

9 During the mating season, how many eggs does a female tokay lay?

10 What year was the tokay gecko included in Appendix II of CITES?

Answers 1. About 72 2. They lick them 3. About 2,000 4. A tokay can cast off its tail 5. It is a vertical slit 6. By rubbing sacs in their throats together 7. 3 to 6 months 8. 0.9 pounds (400 g) 9. She lays two eggs each month 10. 2019

Key Words

adaptations: changes in animals that help them survive in their environment

ambushing: making a surprise attack

camouflage: the ability to hide by matching one's surroundings

diurnal: active during the day and asleep during the night

habitats: places where a plant or animal lives in nature

invasive species: a species of plant or animal not native to an area that is harmful to the environment in that area

invertebrates: animals that do not have backbones

lizards: scaly-skinned reptiles, usually distinguished from snakes by their four legs and external ear openings

mammals: warm-blooded animals that have hair or fur and nurse their young

nocturnal: active at night

populations: groups of individuals of the same species living and interbreeding within a given area

predators: animals that live by killing other animals for food

prey: animals that are hunted by other animals for food

pupils: openings in eyes that control the amount of light that enters

reptiles: air-breathing animals that have scales and a backbone. Their body temperature changes with the temperature around them.

species: a group of animals that share similar features and can reproduce with each other

Index

Get the best of both worlds.

AV2 bridges the gap between print and digital.

The expandable resources toolbar enables quick access to content including **videos**, **audio**, **activities**, **weblinks**, **slideshows**, **quizzes**, and **key words**.

Animated videos make static images come alive.

Resource icons on each page help readers to further **explore key concepts**.

Published by Lightbox Learning Inc.
276 5th Avenue, Suite 704 #917
New York, NY 10001
Website: www.openlightbox.com

Names: Watt, E. Melanie, author.
Title: Tokay gecko / E. Melanie Watt.
Description: New York, NY : Lightbox Learning Inc., [2025] | Series: Animals of the night | Includes index. | Audience: Grades 2-3
Identifiers: LCCN 2024014228 (print) | LCCN 2024014229 (ebook) | ISBN 9798874504762 (library binding) | ISBN 9798874511050 (ebook) | ISBN 9798874504786 (other ebook)
Subjects: LCSH: Tokay gecko--Juvenile literature. | Geckos--Juvenile literature.
Classification: LCC QL666.L245 W38 2025 (print) | LCC QL666.L245 (ebook) | DDC 597.95/2--dc23/eng/20240401
LC record available at https://lccn.loc.gov/2024014228
LC ebook record available at https://lccn.loc.gov/2024014229

Printed in Guangzhou, China
1 2 3 4 5 6 7 8 9 0 28 27 26 25 24

062024
101123

Project Coordinator: John Willis
Art Director: Terry Paulhus
Designer: Mandy Christiansen

Photo Credits
Every reasonable effort has been made to trace ownership and to obtain permission to reprint copyright material. The publisher would be pleased to have any errors or omissions brought to its attention so that they may be corrected in subsequent printings. The publisher acknowledges Getty Images, Alamy, Minden Pictures, Shutterstock, and Wikimedia Commons as its primary image suppliers for this title.